American Rondeau

poems by

Carmine G. Di Biase

Finishing Line Press
Georgetown, Kentucky

American Rondeau

alla memoria di mio nonno,
Alberico Di Biase,
musicista e poeta

ACKNOWLEDGMENTS

"His Own Wine," *South Florida Poetry Journal* (August, 2017)
"Forewarnings," *South Florida Poetry Journal* (February, 2019)
"American Rondeau," *South Florida Poetry Journal* (May, 2019)
"Sublimation," *La Piccioletta Barca* (June, 2020)
"The Forest Cabin," *The Road Not Taken: a Journal of Formal Poetry* (Spring, 2020)
"Muzzled," *South Florida Poetry Journal* (June, 2020)
"The Next Election," *Covid and Poetry* (December, 2020)
"Elegy to an Iceberg" and "The Barbarians," *La Piccioletta Barca* (February, 2021)
"The Sound of Violets by Centennial Bridge," *Italian Americana* (Winter, 2021)
"This Task and That" and "Elegy to a Cyclist," *The Vincent Brothers Review* (May, 2021)
"Skeletons" and "To Warm My Bones," *Scapegoat Review* (Winter, 2021)

Publisher: Leah Huete de Maines
Editor: Christen Kincaid
Cover Art: Anita H. Stewart
Author Photo: Carmine G. Di Biase
Cover Design: Elizabeth Maines McCleavy

Order online: www.finishinglinepress.com
also available on amazon.com

Author inquiries and mail orders:
Finishing Line Press
PO Box 1626
Georgetown, Kentucky 40324
USA

Table of Contents

Roman Rondeau

That old stone space has lost its wooden floor.
Strewn with *harena*, dry sand for wet gore,
it gave the crowd a clean, staged kill. We know,
now, all the corridors of fear below,
the slave's close walls, the lion's cage next door.

And to know is to be a child no more,
to outgrow the vice of the emperor,
the puerile lust for blood, the noise and glow
        that old stone space has lost.

Grotesque, here on this American shore,
these new fat men who would with glee restore
that savage ignorance of long ago.
In their arenas of glass and steel, no
valor lives, only the borrowed horror
        that old stone space has lost.

The Cellist in Prague

You, climbing up the stairs, and I
coming down: how could I resist the part?
I feigned surprise and put my hand up to my mouth
as if to hush myself, then as we crossed I craned my neck
towards you, almost as if to plead.
And making furrows in my brow, I fixed you
with my upturned gaze and asked, "Are you—"
then stopped with mock restraint.

You smiled, your cheeks aglow with expectation.
That was my cue. "Are you not the cellist
I once met in Prague?" You looked abashed: "Goodness no.
I am the lawyer you are meeting only now."

An experiment it was, and planned quite on the spot
to see if something real might come of make believe.
Now here we are, in the vale of years,
together still and thinking on those stairs again.

"Did you know that day that it was all an act?"
I waited all these years
to ask you this, fearing you might take offense.
How serene you were this morning at your mirror,
putting color on your face with steady hand.
"Of course," you said, then looked up slowly
at me unabashed, and smiled:
"But how could I resist the part?"

Skeletons

Now for these new flowers the final touch, a thick
blanket of this mulch. Its rich tang removes me
to his idle barn where, upstairs, the floorboards—
widely spaced—made me hold my breath.

And his house, the front door open and the back,
his sweet smoke wafting through, carried by the breeze.
"These now are my only tools." He meant his pipe,
stick matches and tobacco jar.

On a cardboard box in the attic a hen,
a tin metal toy. You pushed it down on its
red, spring loaded legs, and out from a hole dropped
the plastic egg, darkened by time.

In the box the smell of former life, the bones:
An ulna and a clavicle, greasy still,
a tibia and one huge femur, its old ball
round, smooth, ready to work again.

They were his daughter's bones. Someone had let her
keep them for her studies of the healing arts.
Next to them her yellowed *Gray's Anatomy,*
her notes in faded fountain pen.

His name was Alessandro, but here they called
him Alex, a name that sounded like a bag
of rattling sticks. Alessandro dances, breathes,
somewhere between the soil and sun.

Iago's Dream

We all heard you gasp, my dear Othello,
when Emilia blurted out my crime. You
gasped again when I sank my knife into
her back, but only I could see your face
grow pale. O how I knew your every hue—
how changeable you were!—from lustrous black
to that day's ashen grey. And no one knew
why, after her last breath, I should refuse
to wag my nimble tongue again.

Take them from behind: that was my way with
Cassio too. He did not see me, crouching
low. How he howled! "My leg is cut in two!"
You seemed to guess why I had made that wound
when you raised high your Spanish sword and said,
"a better never did itself sustain
upon a soldier's thigh." You cut me first
to see if I would bleed, and when I bled
you knew that sword was meant for you.

But poor Emilia knew us both, I fear.
She silenced me with her last wish. "O lay
me by my mistress' side," she said, and had
in death what I would never have in life.
When I lay with Cassio he dreamed, you know,
of Desdemona. Muttering her name
he kissed me hard and rubbed his thigh on mine.
And now I see that, all the while, I thought
of you, Othello, and of me.

This Task and That

Joe's short walk home at dusk is always good,
even in this cold: the snow under foot,
his toes warm in his boots, the day's work done.
And he won't, till tomorrow, have to speak
this baffling English tongue, a sapping task.
This sweetens his way home to wife and child.

He grips tight the toy he bought for the child
when he hears the steps behind him. "No good,"
he thinks, "this drunk's an unexpected task."
"Hey Joe! Wait for me! I have a bad foot!
Listen, I can make us rich! Let me speak!
Give me ten. We'll split five grand when I'm done!"

Joe knows right then and there what must be done.
"Come," he says, "but hospital first. Sick child."
They go in through the front. "You sit. No speak,"
says Joe. "I visit, then give you ten. Good?"
The drunk nods and falls asleep, rests his foot
while Joe takes on this nuisance of a task.

But how to find the words for such a task?
He goes up to the desk; the search is done:
"Sick friend," he says, "disease of brain, bad foot."
He trembles like a timid, guilty child,
but if this trick succeeds, how very good
he'll feel, and less afraid, next time, to speak.

The nurse looks up at him and says, "I'll speak
with the doctor soon. Do not overtask
your poor friend. Let him sleep." "Yes, that is good,"
says Joe, then to himself: "My work is done."
He slips out the back, thinking of his child,
and the snow crunches as it meets his foot.

His supper greets his nose before his foot
lands on his porch, before his wife can speak,
before he hears his chattering red-cheeked child.
Joe must hide the Christmas toy, his last task,
wrap it in his big coat, or be undone
and spoil the myth that makes a young life good.

Foot it through your life, he thinks, face this task
and that, speak when you must, don't be outdone
by drunks, remain a child, be always good.

The Forest Cabin

That morning from the fire tower we saw
one roof top amid the forest below.
Whoever lived there would have come to know
the coyote's shrill night cry, the raven's caw.

It happened there that day, up high, that kiss
that took us through the wilderness of life:
the warm, teeming hills, the dark vales of strife,
the flaming hearth, the dreaded cold abyss.

Today I found a thrush's yolk-stained nest
in tatters on the path. Then, near that lone
cabin, a young buck's carcass, stripped to bone,
unforked antlers in its own hollowed breast.

And the cabin empty, the rock that broke
the glass still there, inside, like some grim joke.

His Own Wine

1.

The muffled sounds of work came from the shop
Across the alley, where men and machines
Made hard metal parts for other machines.
He knew enough words to ask for the huge
Bolt and the nut with steel rods welded fast
On either side. The rest he'd make himself
Out of wood: now, at last, after the time
Of work, of uncomplaining plodding on—
In fields, on cobbled streets, in the Alpine
Cave where, covered in lice, he shook for days
With fever—now, at last, his hair gone white,
He'd make a press: he wanted his own wine.

2.

Sickle in hand in the rich landlord's fields,
The graceful bend of the wheat as the wind
Passed gently through it, the pungent manure,
The peaceful drone of bees that never stung,
A hat for the sun, the salt taste of sweat,
And in his brown satchel, the piece of bread,
The piece of cheese, the flask of bitter wine—
All this he remembered—and the long climb
Home at dusk, first the path, the dirt road next,
And then the cobbles at the edge of town.
Even now, in his old mind, he could feel
That last crooked stone, two steps from his door.

3.

The harder climb began when Europe cracked.
The boots and leggings, the jacket, the great
Plume in his cap: with that, and a long gun,
He marched up the narrow mountain path, eyes
Fixed on every step. "If your fellow slipped,"
He'd say, "you'd watch him fall and disappear.
Or if, like me, he felt too sick to move,
You went ahead and left him there alone.
So came the fever, those days in the cave,
The Austrian soldiers, the prison camp."
These things he'd say with a smile, on his porch
Across the alley from the metal shop.

4.

He'd proposed to his wife in a blunt note
Tucked, in secret, in her closed parasol.
"Well, yes," she said. "You've come back, after all,
And others haven't." So their life began.
With a mouse trap and stale bread she caught birds
And cooked them. She dressed his father's bed sores
Till the end. Then across the sea they went,
To a world unbroken and strange, where one
Could work and buy a house and grow one's food,
Where actions mattered more than words: a new
World in the making, much in need of men
Who knew that life was work, that rest came last.

5.

The noisy town—the bar, the burger joint,
The metal shop, its lathes humming all day—
Had grown around their house, the only one
Left, the yard all garden, a patch of green,
Of red and gold, maroon and purple-black.
She altered the roosters with a worn pair
Of her man's pliers. She twisted the heads
Off rabbits so quickly they hardly bled.
She wept as she did these things; and she said,
One day, as she pulled the skin from an eel
With a ripping sound, "When I die, do not
Forget that this is what I had to do."

6.

From the kitchen window she watched him tote
The huge bolt home and the nut with two rods,
One left, one right. On these he'd slide a long
Pipe to ease his task. Round and round the press
He went, and down came the current of sweet
Pink juice, into the basin first and then
The oaken barrels, three of them, enough
To last a year, enough to soften all
The years of climbing home. Down came the juice,
Its thin white froth dissolving as it crashed
Against the basin's edge, like the sea's foam
Against the rocky firmness of the shore.

The Day the White Gull Swooped

That white gull swooped into the stall and took
a drink of fish blood. The vendor's grave look
pursued the shameless disappearing thief,
then quickly turned to sweet, amused relief.
I laughed out loud and felt inspired to cook.

It had long weighed on me, that stolen book,
till that morning the vendor's awning shook
and, thirsting for its red aperitif,
        that white gull swooped.

I pulled the hidden volume from its nook
that night and laughter nearly overtook
me as I read about the bloody grief
of war and calmly sipped my digestif,
grateful for the day that nature's own crook,
        that white gull, swooped.

To Warm My Bones

A cup of tea for me to warm my bones
And I shall listen to your grief until
The night turns to day and the dove intones
Its plaintive song and dew forms on the sill.

And I shall listen to your grief until
You have no grieving left and you have sung
Your plaintive song and dew forms on the sill
And sleep comes down to still your fretting tongue.

You have no grieving left and you have sung
Till all the demons of your heart have fled,
And sleep comes down to still your fretting tongue.
Now I stand watch, your torments in my head.

Till all the demons of your heart have fled:
This pledge I made to you, and I have kept.
Now I stand watch, your torments in my head,
And weep the same hot tears that you have wept.

This pledge I made to you, and I have kept,
Ends here. Hush now, no one must hear my moans
And weep the same hot tears that you have wept.
A cup of tea for me to warm my bones.

Lavinia's Lament

Take my cold hand, dear girl, between your teeth.
Anoint me with your tongue's still bleeding trunk.
This warm, working hand shall my knife unsheathe
and serve now as the quill does serve the monk.

Anoint me with your tongue's still bleeding trunk.
Your wound, on mine, your outrage must inscribe
and serve now as the quill does serve the monk.
Together thus we shall redeem our tribe.

Your wound, on mine, your outrage must inscribe.
Name, dear, who was it lopped your tender hands.
Together thus we shall redeem our tribe.
I'll learn your signs and follow your commands.

Name, dear, who was it lopped your tender hands,
what coward stole your innocence and fled.
I'll learn your signs and follow your commands.
He shall be cooked and to his parents fed.

What coward stole your innocence and fled?
Groan, speechless girl, flail high your stumps and howl!
He shall be cooked and to his parents fed,
for I will know your consonant and vowel.

Groan, speechless girl, flail high your stumps and howl!
This warm, working hand shall my knife unsheathe,
for I will know your consonant and vowel.
Take my cold hand, dear girl, between your teeth.

The Way to the Lake

The thorns snap back at me as I move
through them, step by halting step.
Harmless punctures on my arms and face
remind me that the way to the lake,
different every spring, takes time, that haste,
in its oldest sense, meant strife.

They call to mind the liver mark that veiled
her face—that girl who worked the fruit drink stall
when I was twelve. From behind that mark an unhurt
spirit charmed her every move: the way she dropped
the cherries in and shook the glass, and pressed
the change into my open palm.

And how unwanted, dusty violins, abused
and marred by time, hide their golden sound till played
again, and then their every scar enchants. The crippled hand
of one collector found Cremona's scattered gems.
Their vulgar owners rushed to trade them for the shine
of gold, and of the new ones in his sack.

Your sculpted cheekbones and your porcelain skin.
That impassive, studied elegance, eyes half closed
and hair wind-blown in the silence of our rooms.
How indifferent was your first hello, and that good-bye,
as if no time at all had passed. What you sought was
elsewhere. Yes, I should have known.

Wafting through this thicket comes the water's smell,
and then, at last, the sudden view: the hushed, still lake,
gleaming in the sun. The heron, hearing me, floats
up from its rotting log with slow, majestic wings.
And on my arms I see the beads of blood
now dark, already hardened in this morning air.

Forewarnings

That half-remembered story from thirty years ago.
Love in a sanatorium,
a beautiful, moribund girl with parchment skin,
a man playing cards at a table raises his voice, coughs out blood
and dies on the spot.
The author, a doctor haunted by what he'd seen, had found
consolation in the telling.

And yesterday at the grocery,
the woman with medicine in her voice.
She planted her cane between us with both hands,
the veins in her forearms black and dark blue.
She stared at me as she gathered herself,
and gasped—I could smell her chemical breath—
"The cocoa. Where do they keep the cocoa?"

And this cold evening, I take the kettle off the fire and see
the tiny new blotch on my hand: a broken capillary, a harmless
rupture. It will resolve itself and vanish
like the ones before have done.
How courteous, this brief forewarning
that the Distinguished Thing, as the Master called it,
plans to visit me as well.

Tomorrow I shall give away these things that have
outlived their use: the rowboat and the guest bed,
the bicycle for two—all of it must go. There will be an
hour, tomorrow, to pace about this quiet house and rein in
all these shards of memory. And tomorrow, at my table, a smoking
cup of chocolate by my side, I shall set them forth
in a proper letter and seal it.

The Broken White Line

Absurd tonight how the broken white line recalls that worm
Dangling slack from the cat when the medicine took effect.
Too many miles behind me, and I'm feeling quite infirm.

This last stretch of road snakes up to a lookout, a wide berm,
Then down to that city, by day a picture of neglect.
Absurd tonight how the broken white line recalls that worm.

Those pale truck-stop eggs, my daily fare, used to make me squirm
At first. They are familiar now, a filth that I expect.
Too many miles behind me, and I'm feeling quite infirm.

Somewhere along this journey I must have caught some vile germ,
Or else it is what Hamlet had, that "stamp of one defect."
Absurd tonight how the broken white line recalls that worm.

A life on wheels will give you time and reason to confirm
And reconfirm that fate is fatal, never incorrect.
Too many miles behind me, and I'm feeling quite infirm.

I must push on, or be pushed out a corpse, like a tape-worm
Dangling from a cat. We live in the world that we infect.
Absurd tonight how the broken white line recalls that worm.
Too many miles behind me, and I'm feeling quite infirm.

Ballad of the German Cannibal

"My name's Herr Meiwes. I have a request.
If interested, kindly reply.
A well-built man is what I want,
Who's ready and willing to die,

Who wouldn't mind being chopped to bits,
And fried in garlic and oil.
Your head, be assured, I'll treat with respect,
And return it straight to the soil."

"My name's Herr Brandes. I've read your request.
The century's out and I'm bored.
If you'll be my hero, I'll be your man,
And offer myself to your sword."

"Good evening, Brandes. So glad you're here!
Allow me to show you in.
The house is large, too large for one.
Our adventure's about to begin!"

How hungry I was before your visit!
How hungry and lonely and cold!
I longed for you—did you long for me?—
Since the time I was eight years old.

"Brandes, please, take twenty of these.
There is no need to suffer.
And drink this down—it's a decent Schnapps.
That picture, yes, was my mother.

"My father? No. Let's not discuss him.
He left when I was one.
Yes, do. Please do undress.
Mein Gott! This will be fun!"

"Oh, Meiwes, look: it's come clean off,
And it hardly hurt at all.
Are you pleased with it? Will it make a meal?
Or is it now too small?"

"I'm not displeased at all, my dear.
It will make a fine hors d'oeuvre.
I'll run along to the kitchen now
And soon have it ready to serve."

How hungry I was before your visit!
How hungry and lonely and cold!
I longed for you—did you long for me?—
Since the time I was eight years old.

"Now chew it up and swallow it down,
And try not to fall asleep.
Of course you're bleeding badly, man,
But this, you know, won't keep.

"There, there, my friend, you've had enough.
Allow me to wipe your face.
And while you bathe I'll read my book
About Americans in space."

"Herr Meiwes, look: I'm ready now,
All ready for the slaughter.
I think I'm losing consciousness.
I can't contain my water."

"Herr Brandes, you are statuesque,
All grey and blue and still:
A marble Caesar vandalized.
I'm ready for the kill!

"Come here, my Brandes, come to me.
We've waited long for this."
"But please, Herr Meiwes, one more thing:
Perhaps a parting kiss?"

I kissed you once and laid you down.
You were—*O Gott!*—spectacular!
Then with my finest kitchen knife
I cut right through your jugular.

How hungry I was before your visit!
How hungry and lonely and cold!
I longed for you—did you long for me?—
Since the time I was eight years old.

I bled you like a suckling pig,
Then carved you into portions.
Your head I buried in the yard,
Your face still in contortions.

Forty pounds of broiled Brandes
Through my bowels did pass.
The world considered this barbaric;
To me it was like Mass.

Two weeks went by before they came
And knocked on my front door:
Forty pounds of you quite gone,
And twenty more in store.

Before they knocked I heard one say,
"Let's hope this Meiwes talks."
They saw your bluish thigh in the fridge,
Nudging a pizza box.

"*Mein Gott!*" said one, quite horrified:
How pale and sick he looked.
And I was dreadfully ashamed, you know,
At the sight of you uncooked!

There's plenty of peace and quiet here,
In my little prison cell.
Soon I'll write the story of my life:
I Am the German Cannibal.

How hungry I was before your visit!
How hungry and lonely and cold!
I longed for you—did you long for me?—
Since the time I was eight years old.

A Deed without a Name

I was good at what I did, until I fell
in love with how my deeds rang out distorted
from the mouths of lesser men. It's true, I carved
a gaping hole into Macdonwald and his innards
steamed as they came out. So, yes, my sword smoked,
but I never cut a man in half, lengthwise,
from the navel to the chin. You, my poor king,
so loved to hear such things that you rewarded us
for lies, and not for what we really did.

Before the first of you arrived that night I had already
put my horse to bed and with my wife prepared
our house for royal guests. My speed earned your
praise but my good horse, I knew, deserved it more.
Then, after all the food and drink and cheer, a fleeting image
of a dagger drew me to your room to kill you in your sleep.
How it hurt, next morning, when Macduff barged in
and bellowed "Murder! Treason!"—as if those names
could hold more than a shred of my intent!

I knew—when you smiled down at me and said, "My worthy
Thane of Cawdor!"—that you owned all my names, and me.
Let me be clear: I never wanted to be king.
My desire could not be clothed in any crown
or robe or any of the words I knew. No, I would elude
determination. Those ironic witches told me so.
I asked them what it was they did, and they
instead told me what I had done in killing you:
"a deed without a name."

But as I said, I fell in love with words,
with how they fix and measure what we think and do
and put it on display, always in haste, and change
the shape of everything they hold. My lady's final
hideous cry, which came too soon, defined her.
And blustering Macduff barged in again to say
I would be monstered on a pole and renamed "tyrant."
So goes the world, dear king, from syllable
to syllable, till our brief candle's out.

Elegy to an Iceberg

(after W.H. Auden's "In Memory of W.B. Yeats")

I.

Great
White shelves
Of old fixed time
Fall from your waning flanks
And crash upon the tepid, rising
Sea, there to float awhile and there to melt,
Dissolved at last by heat of arrogance, rage, and greed.

Small
Wonder
That men in boats
Should now rush out to claim
A fatal northwest passage, not found
But made, by accident, like that passage
Cleared where three roads met, by a fool hoping to make time.

II.

You were there before that Greek took the stage,
Before his race stood up on its hind legs
And learned to rape and steal, find wars to wage,
Suck the world's sweet nectar and sell the dregs.

Yesterday you were majestic still, kissed
The heavens with your gelid peak somewhere
Above the clouds; while here below, the mist
About your base filled pillagers with care.

You—rough, colossal uncut gem—would hide
Your ragged facets, lie in wait, and break
Men's ships to bits. And as the drownlings died
They saw, behind the mist, their last mistake.

You made those rovers part of your museum,
Suspended their contorted forms in ice,
That, ages hence, their heirs might witness them:
The shapes of human error and its price.

III.

Now melt, Colossus, melt.
Their cries are all unfelt.
Spill from your liquid maw
Your relics as they thaw,
And in your ghastly crude
Drown this last, ingrate brood.
Remind them, as they sink,
There's truth in Ovid's ink:
Nothing's lost, nothing's gained,
The world is only changed,
And punishments, in time,
Are sure to fit the crime.

Elegy to a Cyclist
(for Cap'n Dave)

We all got stronger chasing after you.
And if at times you broke away from us
You did it to correct some case of pride
Or vanity or overzealous youth.
"O to be sixteen!" said one tired rider
When an upstart surged ahead and dropped us.
You, white hair and all, took flight and caught him.
"Or sixty!" said I, as you both vanished
Round a bend. But today you broke away
For good, and my knees buckled at the news.

We first met on that mountain, at the top,
You, all stern, standing by your yellow bike,
Your friend by his, a lustrous cherry red.
How they gleamed that day under that bright sun!
He smiled. He knew I could not turn away:
"Come ride with us someday," he said. "We'll show
You round." And you said, "Yeah man, get a bike."
So began my second life among good
Friends who understood that pleasure was not
Free but came from work, selflessness, and pain.

You were the quiet, understated one,
The strongest: the example shining pure.
From you we learned that bragging was for fools,
That to suffer as one was our high goal.
We all took our turns up front, cutting through
The wind and rain, sparing the ones behind.
"Car left! Car right! Car back! Dog up ahead!"
How many times we called those warnings out,
Even when no damned dog or car was there.
"I've got your back" was what we really meant.

A rite of passage was Twin Churches Road.
You and your friend on the cherry bike fooled
Me into feeling proud. You let me pull
The group till I could pull no more, then stood
Up on your bikes and hammered past with all
Your strength, feigning grave, cruel, unsmiling looks.

I laughed as your friend shrank to a red dot
In the distance, you to a yellow dot.
Behind me one spent rider, breathing hard,
Forced out one short laugh, and gasped, "Cap'n Dave!"

It was like flying, rolling down those hills
At speeds that tempted fate, or over flats
When some rare blessed tailwind pushed us on.
Such were our brief rewards. The cost was steep:
The long, slow climbs that turned our legs to mush,
And on the flats, almost always, some vile
Headwind that in hot summer filled our lungs
With steam and in the winter made us feel
The chill of death. You showed us how to prove
That we were worthy of the joy of flight.

Once, along a wooded road, a lone hawk
Followed us, low overhead, for one full
Minute. His shadow covered your whole back.
Another time three does pranced gracefully
Beside us, long enough to fill us all
With admiration. "Ease up," said your friend,
"They're no different. They want to be with us."
There was deep consolation in those hills,
Unrolling in shades of green, shades of brown,
Waves of easy colors that washed one's soul.

"It'll hurt your feelings," you said one day
About the awful wreckage caused by time.
And last summer, before a ride, you looked
Straight at me and said, "I'm falling apart."
Today you broke away from us for good.
"May he rest in peace now," your friends will say.
At peace, no doubt, you are, but at rest? You?
You're chasing down some upstart in the sky.
Come down, some sunny day, and ride with us,
And lay your winged shadow on our backs.

Us and Them

They burned it all: the crime is done.
Their poison now obscures the sun
and floats up from the ocean floor,
pitch black, to gather on this shore.
And we thought life had just begun.

Their leader sees us on the run,
hand in hand, falling one by one,
and murmurs smugly to his whore
                     they burned it all.

Amid the tar and sand a nun,
serene, unmoving, says, "They've won,
or so they think. They'll grope, before
this bane seeps under their own door,
for just such hands, but they'll find none:
                     they burned it all."

The Barbarians
>   (after C. P. Cavafy's "Expecting the Barbarians")

"The barbarians are coming," said the orator, and his deep voice
>   boomed and resounded, and the frightened citizens
>   fortified their city walls.

Every seventh day at noon they rehearsed the dreaded event:
>   the siren sounded and they stopped their work and scurried
>   to the bunker, singing songs in praise of their grey-haired emperor.

But no barbarians came.

The orator spoke again, his voice booming and resounding until
>   the citizens were all afraid and of one mind: the barbarians
>   were coming soon, the senate must make new laws,
>   seek out the menace beyond the city walls and make war
>   there, far from the city.

And the senate made new laws, and the orator, now in a loving
>   voice, assured the citizens that someday the barbarians
>   would all be destroyed.

And a new emperor, with tar black hair, was crowned, and he saw
>   that the citizens were no longer afraid. Now, at the sound
>   of the siren, they went to the bunker slowly, some of them
>   singing but not with the old spirit, others grumbling or
>   muttering the names—Rats! Vermin! Dogs!—by which they
>   had come to know the barbarians.

Yet no citizen, not even the soldiers who returned with wounds,
>   had ever seen a barbarian.

Another year passed, and the emperor grew worried. The citizens,
>   tired of waiting for the barbarians, began to hurl
>   the filthy names at one another, and at themselves. One day
>   from his turret he saw citizen killing citizen. The next day,
>   down in the forum, he saw the butcher run himself through
>   with his meat knife, as he cried out, "Down with the emperor!"

The orator grew old, his voice now feeble, and still no sign of barbarians.

And the emperor ordered the senate to make new laws again,
    laws that would make the citizens believe in barbarians once more.
    Now, every seventh day at midnight, the soldiers would break
    through one citizen's door and shackle him or kill him, and
    a young new orator, in a shrill, high voice, would declare
    him a barbarian.

The old songs in praise of the emperor were sung again, loudly as before,
    but always in anger now, and only to cover the few meek
    voices calling out for justice.

When his black hair turned white, the emperor looked out from
    his turret and saw that the streets were quiet and untidy:
    a child's toy sword, a young girl's gown, one sleeve torn away,
    an old man's cane, a sheep's head blackened by flies, the bunker
    door left open and swinging in the wind.

And the emperor asked himself, "Did my people somehow become
    barbarians, or were they always the barbarians they were
    waiting for?"

Muzzled

A sudden, grand reproach last spring for crimes
against the world. They stopped their chattering mouths
behind their masks and hid their bloated pride,
hid their joys, their griefs, hid their love and hate,
put an end to all their violations,
celebrations, funeral orations,
their loud belittling of other nations.
All went home at once, noiselessly, and stowed
away in fear.

Then just as suddenly, the waters cleared.
The finned inhabitants retook their space
and even leapt into the air to dare
their winged counterparts to play once more
at catch me if you can, that deadly game
of old. Down they swooped—now that they could breathe
again and see—and spread their feathers wide
to revel in the rediscovered thrill
of pure, shared fear.

How plain, now, this game's stark rule. All must show
respect, and all must play: outside or in,
the field is everywhere. The chastened, still
holed up this June, are in pajamas day
and night, soft garb for toughs. And muzzled tight,
they know the blameless die with mouths attached
to crude machines. Next month the predator
will leave, or wait, or strut right in. Respect
is three parts fear.

The Next Election
(after W.B. Yeats's "The Second Coming")

Whirling and whirling in the thickening air
The virus does not spare the virulent;
Lungs breathe it in; it enters through the pores;
Sheer treachery is loosed within the veins.
The crown-shaped beast is loosed, and everywhere
The memory of embracing is gone:
The best are all indifferent, while the worst
Burn hot with partisan intensity.

Surely some vaccination is at hand;
Surely the Next Election is at hand.
The Next Election! Hardly are those words out
When the horrid image of *Voter Suppression*
Hovers before me: there, in the usurped White House,
The "bloat king," as Hamlet called him, polishes his gold,
And moves his slow, chafed thighs, while all about him
Flit the shadows of his craven enablers.
Dejection comes again; but now I hope
That two centuries of democracy,
Undone by a spoiled slouch, might find new life
If, unseen and swift, this dread Corona,
Reaching Washington, strips him of his crown.

Sublimation

This is the moment, this, when yesterday
encroaches on tomorrow, holds it fast
and drags it by the neck into the past,
blindfolded through the riches of today.

These warm arms, this free breath, this crystal light:
all this puts me in mind of that cold steel
gauntlet clenched tight around my throat. I feel
the grip, even now, of that coming night.

And yet this dread, lodged deep in time's morass,
is but a moment, a mere dread in time,
and will not long enjoy its haughty prime
before it too must go this way and pass,

become, indeed, sublime. Dark are the charms
that move this light, this breath, and warm these arms.

The Sound of Violets by Centennial Bridge

It was above my head, that brief exchange
at the covered bridge. He had walked up there alone.
"Bring him here!" he called to her, in the language
of my other life. "This bridge was named to mark
one hundred years of freedom from the English!"

And she, reaching down to me and to the ground
beneath our feet, whispered, "*Vedi qua. Le violette.*"
She wrapped her lips around that name
and made it vibrate through her arm and hand,
and into mine, her free hand pointing at the thin
blue petals, trembling in a momentary breeze.

She walked me up to that old bridge, and we stepped
into its dark and wooden hollow. What a rumble there,
the sound of water coursing fast below. And how his voice
resounded off the knotty sideboards: "This is nothing!
The Romans built much bigger ones! And used cement
two thousand years ago!"

"Let's go back down," she said, "down to the grass,"
and her grip tightened. "We'll have the sandwiches I made."
Not once, since then, have I seen blue petals
and not heard again "*le violette*" and not seen again those lips,
wrapped perfectly around that sound.

Prospero's Staff

The twangling of a thousand lutes and viols ravished
that unlettered islander, took him to the land of sleep and dream.
From his hard, dewy bed he saw a firmament engorged with riches
ready to rain down upon him, bathe him, turn him to a vapor that might
rise high and wrap itself around some dark celestial gem.
How he cried when he awoke. How he longed
to dream again.

His newfound friend, the butler, awed him with a humbler
magic, carved a bottle from a log and, with the jester, showed him
how to quaff the wine from that buoyant lucky butt on which the keeper
of the buttery had floated safely onto shore. Theirs was the drunken
dream of rape and stolen power. Knock a nail into the head
of the magician? Nail his daughter too?
O comedy!

And was not that magician, the ousted duke, forced, with his
child and book, into a rotten carcass of a butt? His vengeance
took twelve years to ripen. No vulgar wrecking of the proud usurper's
boat but an undoing, a reversing of the magic of floatation:
stave pulled apart from stave, butt end from butt end slowly gapped.
"We split!" one sailor said. Their boat leaked like
an unstanched wench.

That magician's daughter, herself a leaking vessel,
became the crisis. Her stranded prince hauled logs for her, embraced his
labor, and she pitied him. "If you'll sit down," she said, "I'll bear your logs
the while." Bear them indeed, and bear more princes—that too a kind of magic.
Unlike the islander, her patient log man earned her hand
through toil, yet he would have his way with her
and stanch the wench.

"We split!" that sailor said, not knowing the magician
well could split a log, make staves unbowed and true, bend them to his will
for boats and butts and lutes and viols. And once he too had stanched a wench.
Perfected in his art, he found the choicest log and split from its hard core
his staff, alive and black, the stave of staves. It was with this
he freed his airy fancy, spreading wide
the cloven pine.

The final wonder—after all the rage and lust, all
the remorse—was to see that disassembled boat, now tight and yare
again, float back to the world of made things, leaving the staff behind, cracked
in two and buried, the book drowned deep in a filthy pool, the islander
alone, the airy fancy wanting work. The vision gone,
what remained? Blank paper, wet ink, a quill,
a wooden stage.

American Rondeau

I nearly overlooked this arrowhead
tonight. See how it glows, like Mars, faint red
under this moon, this piece of silica
that long ago tore through the viscera
of some poor beast on which the hunter fed.

Suspended in this blackness, all outspread
against the stars, the quickening homebred
objects float, a teeming cornucopia
                    I nearly overlooked:

Top hats, guns, trombones, a child's painted sled,
clocks, chrome bumpers, blue jeans with yellow thread,
the gleaming marquee of a cinema—
the dream-time history of America,
an unfurled picture scroll above my head
                    I nearly overlooked.

Carmine Di Biase's poems have appeared in *South Florida Poetry Journal, The Road Not Taken, La Piccioletta Barca, Italian Americana, The Vincent Brothers Review, Scapegoat Review* and other journals. His reviews and translations appear occasionally in the *Times Literary Supplement*. A recent issue of *L'Anello che non tiene: The Journal of Modern Italian Literature* published his translations of thirteen poems by Cesare Pavese. Di Biase writes on Shakespeare and modern English and Italian literature. He has edited and translated, from the manuscript, *The Diary of Elio Schmitz: Scenes from the World of Italo Svevo*, which appeared in 2013. In 2015 Di Biase edited and introduced *"Oh! Mio Vecchio William!": Italo Svevo and His Shakespeare*, a collection of essays by various scholars who explore Shakespeare's influence on Italy's most important modern novelist. At the moment, Di Biase is translating Carlo Collodi's little known sequel to *Pinocchio*, which will probably bear the title *Pipì, the Pink Chimpanzee*. Di Biase also serves as dramaturg for The Shakespeare Project, a non-profit organization that offers eight consecutive, professional performances of one Shakespeare play every year, free of charge, aimed mainly at underserved Alabama high school students but open to the general public as well. He is Distinguished Professor of English Emeritus at Jacksonville State University. In his spare time, he restores old violins, plays in local orchestras, and tries to make life easier for his wife, who teaches music and is principal cellist for the Gadsden Symphony Orchestra.